I0103819

Alfred R. Wallace

Vaccination

Proved Useless & Dangerous

Alfred R. Wallace

Vaccination
Proved Useless & Dangerous

ISBN/EAN: 9783337565039

Printed in Europe, USA, Canada, Australia, Japan

Cover: Foto ©Andreas Hilbeck / pixelio.de

More available books at **www.hansebooks.com**

VACCINATION

Proved Useless & Dangerous

FROM FORTY-FIVE YEARS OF REGISTRATION STATISTICS.

ALFRED R. WALLACE, LL.D.

TO MEMBERS OF PARLIAMENT

AND OTHERS.

Forty-five years of Registration Statistics, proving Vaccination to be both useless and dangerous.

In Two Parts.

ALFRED R. WALLACE, LL.D.

SECOND EDITION.

WITH CORRECTIONS, NOTES, AND AN APPENDIX.

By ALEXANDER WHEELER.

London:

E. W. ALLEN, 4 AVE MARIA LANE.

1889.

Forty-five years of Registration Statistics.

PART I.

Small-pox Mortality and Vaccination.

HAVING been led to enquire for myself as to the effects of Vaccination in preventing or diminishing Small-pox, I have arrived at results as unexpected as they appear to me to be conclusive. The question is one which affects our personal liberty as well as the health and even the lives of thousands; it therefore becomes a duty to endeavour to make the truth known to all, and especially to those who, on the faith of false or misleading statements, have enforced the practice of vaccination by penal laws.

I propose now to establish the following four statements of fact, by means of the only official statistics which are available; and I shall adopt a mode of presenting those statistics as a whole, which will render them intelligible to all. These statements are:

(1.)—That during the forty-five years of the Registration of deaths and their causes, Small-pox mortality has very slightly diminished, while an exceedingly severe Small-pox epidemic occurred within the last twelve years of the period.

(2.)—That there is no evidence to show that the slight decrease of Small-pox mortality is due to vaccination.

(3.)—That the severity of Small-pox as a disease has not been mitigated by vaccination.

(4.)—That several inoculable diseases have increased to an alarming extent coincidently with enforced vaccination.

The first, second, and fourth propositions will be proved from the Registrar-General's Reports from 1838 to 1882; and I shall make the results clear and indisputable, by presenting the figures for the whole period in the form of diagrammatic curves, so that no manipulation of them, by taking certain years for comparison, or by dividing the period in special ways, will be possible.

DIAGRAM I

Deaths in London per Million Living from Small Pox and from the Chief other Zymotic Diseases except Cholera

Lower Line Small Pox   Dotted Line Typhus &c.   Upper Line Zymotic Diseases.

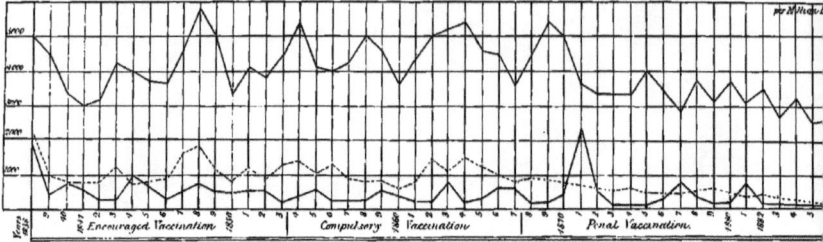

per Million

Encouraged Vaccination   Compulsory Vaccination   Penal Vaccination.

DIAGRAM II.

Deaths in England and Wales per Million Living from Small Pox and from the Chief other Zymotic Diseases except Cholera.

Lower Line Small Pox   Dotted Line Official Vaccination   Upper Line Zymotic Diseases.

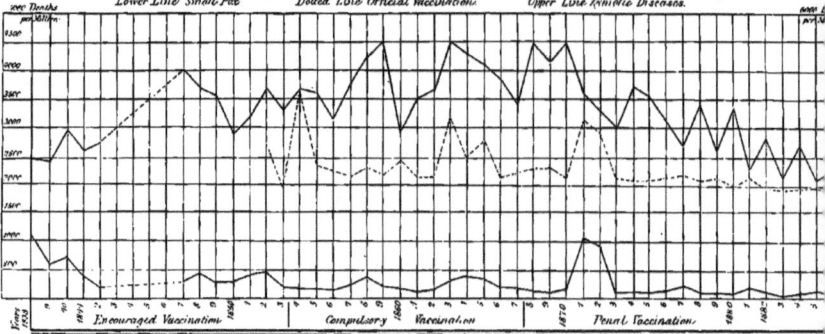

Deaths per Million

Encouraged Vaccination   Compulsory Vaccination   Penal Vaccination.

NOTE. The Official Vaccination Line is per 100,000 of the living Population

The diagrams show, in each case, not the absolute mortality but the deaths per million living, a method which eliminates the increase of population and gives true comparative results.

VACCINATION HAS NOT DIMINISHED SMALL-POX.

DIAGRAM I. exhibits* the deaths from Small-pox, in LONDON, for every year from 1838 to 1882, while an upper line exhibits the deaths from the other principal zymotic diseases given in the Registrar-General's Annual Summary for 1882, (except Cholera, which is only an occasional epidemic,) namely,—Scarlet fever and Diphtheria, Measles, Whooping Cough, Typhoid and other fevers, and Diarrhœa. A dotted line between these shows the mortality from fevers of the Typhoid class.†

The first thing clearly apparent in this diagram, is the very small diminution of Small-pox

---

* The Diagrams in the First Edition stopped at 1882. In this Edition the later years are added without variation of the text, which these later years do but accentuate. Complaint has been made of this presentment. It is the most accurate that can be made. The favorite method of averaging in such a manner as to take all the sharp lines from the curves, totally obscures the epidemic nature of the disease of Small-pox, its great characteristic feature. No truer presentment than that chosen can be adopted. The line of official vaccinations includes, for 1884-5-6, official re-vaccinations, which have not been given since 1872, or the fall would be much more pronounced for these years.—ED.

† From the Registrar-General's Annual Summary of Deaths, etc., in London, 1882. Table 23, p. xxv.

corresponding with the epochs of penal and compulsory vaccination ; while the epidemic of 1871 was the most destructive in the whole period. The average diminution of Small-pox mortality from the first to the second half of the period, is 57 deaths per million per annum. Looking now at the upper curve, we see that the mortality from the chief zymotic diseases has also decreased,* more especially during the last 35 years ; but the decrease of these diseases is not, proportionally, so great, owing to the fact that deaths from Diarrhœa have considerably increased in the latter half of the period.   On the other hand, Typhus and Typhoid fevers have diminished to a much greater extent than Small-pox, as shown by the dotted line on the diagram, the reduced mortality from this cause alone being 382 per million, or more than six times as much as that from Small-pox.   Every one will admit that this remarkable decrease of Typhus,† &c.,

---

* From 1838 to 1853, the average Small-pox death-rate exceeded that of the years 1854 to 1867 by 229 per million living. But the average of the years 1868 to 1886, exceeded that of the years 1854 to 1867 by 46 per million.

† The deaths from Typhus, Enteric, and Fever, 1871-80, were less by 540 per million than in the ten preceding years. The years 1881 to 1886 show a further reduction, as compared with 1871 to 1880, of 125 per million living. — ED.

is due to more efficient sanitation, greater
personal attention to the laws of health, and
probably also to more rational methods of
treatment. But all these causes of amelioration
have certainly had their effect on Small-pox ;
and as the mortality from that disease has
not equally diminished, there is probably some
counteracting cause at work. So far, therefore,
from there being any proof that vaccination
has diminished Small-pox in London, the
tendency of the Registrar-General's facts, (and
there are no other facts which are trustworthy,)
is to show that some counteracting cause has
prevented general sanitation from acting on
this disease as it has acted on Typhus, and
that cause may, possibly, be vaccination itself.

We will now turn to DIAGRAM II., which
gives a representation of similar statistics for
England and Wales,* except that unfortunately
there is a blank in the record for 1843-46, in
which years the Registrar-General informs us,
"the causes of death were not distinguished."
Here too we perceive a similar decrease in
Small-pox mortality, broken by the tremendous
epidemic of 1871-2, while the other chief
zymotic diseases represented by the higher

---

* From the Registrar-General's Annual Report, 1882. Table 32, p. xliii.

line, show more irregularity, but a considerable recent decrease. For all England, as for London, the tables show us that Typhoid fevers have decreased far more than Small-pox, (but for clearness the curve of Typhus is omitted,) and we have, therefore, again, no reason for imputing the decrease in Small-pox to vaccination. But we may go further than this negative statement, for we have, fortunately, a means of directly testing the alleged efficacy of vaccination. The eleventh Annual Report of the Local Government Board gives a table of the number of successful vaccinations, at the expense of the Poor Rate, in England and Wales, from 1852 to 1881. From the figures of this table I have calculated the numbers in proportion to the population of each year, and have exhibited the result in the dotted line on my DIAGRAM II.; and to this I beg to direct the reader's attention, since it at once dispels some oft-repeated erroneous statements.*

In the first place we see that, instead

---

* I have examined every Report of the Local Government Board, with the intention of giving the total vaccinations for the whole period embraced in this Diagram II. But the total vaccinations are not tabulated, and are only given in the text for the years since 1872. Hence the official vaccinations only appear here, with such vaccinations as are tabulated. —ED.

of vaccination having increased since the
enforcement of penal laws, it has actually
diminished; so that the statement so often
made by official apologists for vaccination, and
repeated by SIR LYON PLAYFAIR in his speech
to the House of Commons, June, 1883,—that the
progressive efficiency of legal vaccination has
diminished Small-pox, *is absolutely untrue,
since there has been a decrease rather than
an increase of "efficient vaccination."* * A

---

* It is curious that even the Registrar-General appears to be
ignorant of the fact that, official vaccination has not increased in
efficiency since the penal laws came into force. In his Report for
1880, p. xxii., he says—"These figures show conclusively that,
coincidently with the gradual extension of the practice of vaccination,
there has been a gradual and notable decline in the mortality from
Small-pox at all ages." As, however, there has not been shown to
have been any such "gradual extension of the practice of vaccination,"
but, so far as official records go, just the reverse, the whole argument
falls to the ground! It is true that this curve does not exhibit the numbers
of the vaccinated population, which there is no means of arriving at.

MR. MARSON, the Surgeon of the Small-pox Hospital, told the Select
Committee, 1871, answer 4,190 :—"The public are pretty largely
vaccinated now, and will be more so every year, I should think as time
goes on. There is one point which has not been very clearly brought
forward this morning, and that is the increase of Small-pox after vaccination
year after year. When I first went to the hospital, 35 years since, from
1835 to 1845, the admission of patients into the Small-pox hospital was
44 per cent. of Small-pox after vaccination; from 1845 to 1855, 64 per
cent.; from 1855 to 1865, 78 per cent.; and during 1863 and 1864, 83
and 84 per cent. Those are patients who have been vaccinated." The
line of official vaccination in the diagram, shows that MR. MARSON was
mistaken as to the amount of public vaccination, and that it was a larger
incidence of Small-pox among the vaccinated he was witnessing; not the
result of extension of vaccination.—ED,

temporary increase in the number of vaccinations always takes place during an epidemic
of Small-pox, or when an epidemic is feared ;
but an examination of the curve of vaccination
does not support the statement that it checks
the epidemic. On careful inspection it will
be seen that on three separate occasions
a considerable *increase* in vaccinations was
followed by an *increase* of Small-pox. Let
the reader look at the Diagram, and note
that in 1863 there was a very great number
of vaccinations, followed in 1864 by an *increase*
in Small-pox mortality. Again, the number of
vaccinations steadily rose from 1866 to 1869,
yet in 1870-71 Small-pox mortality increased; and
yet again, in 1876 an *increase* in vaccinations
was followed by an *increase* of Small-pox deaths.
In fact, if the dotted line showed *inoculation*
instead of *vaccination*, it might be used to
prove that inoculation caused an increase of
Small-pox. I only maintain, however, that it
does *not* prove that vaccination diminishes the
mortality from the disease. During the panic
caused by the great epidemic of 1871-2, vaccinations rose enormously, and declined as rapidly
the moment the epidemic passed away, but there
is nothing whatever to show that the increased

vaccinations had any effect on the disease, which ran its course and then died out like other epidemics.

It has now been proved from the only complete series of official records that exist :—

(1.)—That Small-pox has not decreased so much or so steadily as Typhus and allied fevers.

(2.)—That the diminution of Small-pox mortality coincides with a *diminished*, instead of an increased efficiency of official vaccination.

(3.)—That one of the most severe epidemics of Small-pox on record, within the period of accurate statistics, occurred after 33 years of official, compulsory, and penal vaccination.

These three groups of facts give no support to the assertion that vaccination has diminished Small-pox mortality ; and it must always be remembered that we have actually no other extensive body of statistics on which to found our judgment. The utility or otherwise of vaccination is purely a question of statistics. It remains for us to decide, whether we will be guided by the only trustworthy statistics we possess, or continue blindly to accept the dogmas of an interested and certainly not infallible body of professional men, who once upheld inoculation as strongly as they now uphold vaccination.

SMALL-POX HAS NOT BEEN MITIGATED
BY VACCINATION.

It is often asserted that, although vaccination is not a complete protection against Small-pox, yet it diminishes the severity of the disease, and renders it less dangerous to those who take it. This assertion is sufficiently answered by the proof above given, that it has *not* diminished Small-pox mortality; but more direct evidence can be adduced.

The best available records show that, the proportion of deaths to Small-pox cases is the same *now, although a large majority of the population are vaccinated,* as it was a century ago before vaccination was discovered. DR. JURIN, in 1723; the London Small-pox Hospital Reports, 1746-63; DR. LAMBERT, 1763; and REES' Cyclopædia, 1779; give numbers varying from 16·5 to 25·3 as the per-centage of mortality among Small-pox patients in hospitals;—*the average of the whole being* 18·8 *per cent.*

Now for the epoch of vaccination. MR. MARSON, 1836-51, and the Reports of the London, Homerton, Deptford, Fulham, and Dublin Small-pox Hospitals, between 1870 and 1880, give numbers varying from 14·26 to 21·7 as the deaths per cent. of Small-pox patients, *the average being* 18·5. And this, be it remembered, under the improved treatment and hygiene of the nineteenth as compared with the eighteenth century.

These figures not only demonstrate the falsehood of the oft-repeated assertion that vaccination mitigates Small-pox, but they go far to prove the very opposite—that the disease has been rendered more intractable by it; or how can we account for the mortality among Small-pox patients being almost exactly the same now as a century ago, notwithstanding the great advance of medical science and the improvements in hospitals and hospital treatment? *

* The following authorities have been examined for the facts and figures of this section.

DR. JURIN (18,066 cases) and DR. LAMBERT (72 cases) given in "Analyse et Tableau de l'influence de la Petite Verole ; par E. E. DUVILLARD. Paris, 1806." (pp. 112, 113.)

London Small-pox Hospitals (6,454 cases) given in "An account of the Rise, Progress, and State of the Hospitals for relieving poor people afflicted with the Small Pox, and for Inoculation," appended to "A Sermon preached before the President and Officers of the Hospital . . . . by the Bishop of Lincoln. London, 1763."

REES' Cyclopædia, 1779, Vol. 2, Art. INOCULATION Col. INP. par. 5, (extract). "From a general calculation it appears that, in the Hospitals for Small-pox and Inoculation, 75 die out of 400 patients having the distemper in the natural way."

Total cases before Vaccination, 24,994.

MR. MARSON, Resident Surgeon to the Small-pox and Vaccination Hospital, London, (5,652 cases) ; given in the Blue Book on The History and Practice of Vaccination, 1857, p. 18.

SMALL-POX IN THE ARMY AND NAVY.

Here we have a crucial test of the efficacy
or uselessness of vaccination. Our Soldiers
and Sailors are vaccinated and re-vaccinated
in accordance with the most stringent official
regulations. They are exceptionally strong
and healthy men, in the prime of life, and
if vaccination is of any use, Small-pox should
be almost unknown among them, and *no*

London Hospitals, 1870-72, (14,808 cases); in the Report of a Committee
of the Managers of the Metropolitan Asylum District, July 1872, p. 5.

London Hospitals, 1876-80, (15,172 cases); in a letter to *The Times*
of November 8th, 1879, from W. F. JEBB, Clerk to the Metropolitan
Asylum District.

Homerton, (5,479 cases); from the Report of the Committee, 1877.

Deptford, (3,185 cases); from the Report of the Medical Superintendent, 1881.

Fulham, (1,752 cases); from the Report of the Medical Superintendent,
1881.

Dublin, (2,404 cases); from the Annual Report of the Committee, 1880.

Total cases after Vaccination, 48,451.

The extracted figures and per-centages have been all carefully verified,
and the averages have been obtained by dividing the total number of deaths
multiplied by 100, by the total number of cases.

I have thought it best to leave these notes unaltered. They are not
affected by more recent experience, excepting in this way:—That the great
extension of our hospital accommodation involves a much larger number of
mild cases being admitted. Objection has been taken to JURIN'S figures.
JURIN, it must be remembered, was trying to induce people to accept
artificial Small-pox by inoculation, and he gives his figures to show the
great fatality of Small-pox taken in the ordinary way by infection. He
would therefore certainly not err in making it too mild. The total
experience of the Metropolitan Asylums Board, up to the issue of the last
report to the managers, is given in the Appendix.—ED.

soldier or sailor should ever die of it. They
are in fact often spoken of as a "perfectly
protected population." Now let us see what
are the facts.

A Return has been issued to the House of
Commons, "Small-pox (Army and Navy),"
dated "August, 1884," giving the mean strength,
the number of deaths from Small-pox, and the
ratio per thousand in each service for the twenty-
three years 1860-82. An examination of this
Return shows us that there has not been a single
year without two or more deaths in the Army,
and only two years without deaths in the Navy.
Comparing the Return on "Vaccination, Mortality,"
No. 433, issued by the House of Commons in
1877, we find that, in the twenty-three years
1850-72, (the latest there given,) there were many
years in which no adult Small-pox deaths were
recorded for a number of large towns of from
100,000 to 270,000 inhabitants. Liverpool had
none in 3 of the years, Birmingham and Sun-
derland in 7, Bradford and Sheffield in 8, Halifax
in 9, Dudley in 10, while Blackburn and Wolver-
hampton were each totally without adult Small-
pox mortality for 11 out of the 23 years!

It is true that the cases are not strictly
comparable, because for these towns we have

only deaths of persons aged 20 and upwards
given separately, whereas the ages of the
Army and Navy range chiefly from about 17 to
45. But, considering the extremely unsanitary
state of many of these towns, and their great
preponderance in freedom from Small-pox, there
is clearly no room left for the alleged effect of *re-vaccination* in securing to our soldiers and sailors
immunity from the disease.

But let us now look at the averages for the
whole series of years, as affording the best and
only reliable test. On working these out carefully
I find the mean Small-pox mortality for the 23
years to be, in the Army 82·96, which we may
call 83 per million, and in the Navy* 157 per
million. Unfortunately no materials exist for an
exact comparison of these rates with those of the
civil population ; but with much labour I have
made the best comparison I can arrive at. From
the Census General Report, 1881, and the Reports
of the Registrar-General for the same 23 years
as are included in the Army and Navy Return,

---

* The 45th Report of the Registrar-General, (Tables 63 and 4,) gives 25
Small-pox deaths among 195,937 British Merchant Seamen in 1882. This
is at the rate of 127 per million, against the above 157 for the Navy. We
have no reason to believe that re-vaccination is common in the merchant
service. In the Navy, therefore, the influence of re-vaccination appears to
be hurtful rather than beneficial.—ED.

I have been able to ascertain the Small-pox mortality of males in England and Wales between the years 15 and 55, taken as best representing those of the two services ; and the result is a mean Small-pox death rate of 176 per million.*

It will be observed that this is but little more than the Navy mortality, though more than double that of the Army, and the question arises, to what is the difference due. And first, why is the Small-pox mortality in the Navy nearly double that of the Army? The

* The following are the data on which this calculation is founded :—

In the General Report of the last Census, Table 14, p. 89, the numbers of males at successive ages are given for the three last Censuses—1861, 1871, and 1881. By a simple calculation it is found that the number of males of all ages is to that of males aged 15—55 in the proportion of 1 to ·528.

Table 4, p. 78, of the same Census Report, gives the male population for the middle of each of the 23 years included in the Army and Navy Return. The mean of these numbers is 11,167,500 ; and this sum, multiplied by the factor ·528, gives 5,896,500 for the average male population of the ages 15—55 for those years.

From the tables of "Causes of Death at different Periods of Life" in the twenty-three successive Reports of the Registrar-General, 1860-1882, I have extracted the deaths from Small-pox of males aged 15—55, the mean annual value of which is 1,041 ; and this number, divided by the number of millions in the corresponding population (5·8965), gives the death-rate per million = 176.

The limit of age, 15—55, has been taken because the General Report of the Census of 1881, Table 40, gives, for the Army and Navy, 7,530 men over 45, and 28,834 under 20 years of age.

The Small-pox death-rate for same ages, England and Wales, for the years 1850 to 1870, was only 109 per million. Supplement to 35th Report, Table 2, p. 2. The enormous increase is due to the epidemics since 1870.—ED.

B

regulations as to re-vaccination are the same in both, and are in both rigidly enforced, and the men are pretty equal in stamina and general health. The cause must therefore be in the different conditions of life of the two services; and it seems to me a probable supposition, that the difference arises chiefly from the less efficient ventilation and isolation which are possible on board ship as compared with Army Hospitals.*

The general mortality of the Navy from disease appears (from the Registrar-General's Report, 1882, Tables 59 and 65,) to be considerably less than that of the Army, so that the greater mortality from Small-pox must be due to some special conditions. But whatever these are, the conditions of the civil population are certainly much worse. Two-thirds of the families inhabiting Glasgow live in houses of one or two rooms only, and many other towns, including London, are probably not much better. Under such conditions, and with the

---

* An Officer of the Royal Marine Artillery, of great experience, confirms this view. He assures me that isolation is absolutely impossible on board a ship of war. But if this is the explanation of the phenomenon, it is itself a proof of the complete inefficacy of re-vaccination, which not only does not protect men from *catching* Small-pox, but allows them to *die* of it quite as much as—and, allowing something for the superiority of sanitation, even more than—the adult civil population, only partially vaccinated and hardly ever re-vaccinated !

low vitality induced by insufficient food, over-
work, and bad air, we should expect the Small-pox
mortality of our civil population to be very much
greater than that of the picked class of sailors
who enjoy ample food, fresh air, and medical
attendance. Where then is the alleged "full
security" afforded by re-vaccination, and how are
we to characterise the statements circulated at
the expense of the public, that "Small-pox is
almost unknown in the Army and Navy?" * If
we are to draw a legitimate conclusion from
the facts, it is, that the re-vaccination to which
our soldiers and sailors are subjected, renders
Small-pox more fatal when it attacks them, for
thus only can we explain the large mortality

---

* The following are a few of these assertions. The italics are to call
attention to the essential words of each statement.

The "Lancet," of March 1st, 1879, says :—"Vaccination needs to be
repeated well once in a lifetime, *and then the immunity is almost absolute.*"

The Medical Officer of the General Post Office says, in a circular
dated June, 1884.—"The *only means* of securing protection against
Small-pox is by re-vaccination . . . . it is desirable, *in order to obtain
full security*, that the operation should be repeated at a later period of life."

In the tract on "Small-pox and Vaccination" issued by the National
Health Society, and now being widely circulated at the expense of the
ratepayers, with the sanction of the Local Government Board, we find
this statement :—" Every Soldier and Sailor is re-vaccinated ; the result
is that *Small-pox is almost unknown in the Army and Navy*, even amid
surrounding epidemics."

The above statements are proved by the Official Returns now issued
to be absolutely untrue, and must have been ignorantly and recklessly
made without any adequate basis of fact,

among picked healthy men under constant medical supervision, and living under far better sanitary conditions than the mass of the civil population.

One other mode of comparison can be made, showing that even the Army Small-pox death-rate is but little better than that of some large towns, during the same period. The rate per million for the adult population, between the ages 15 and 55, on an average of the years 1860-82 for five very large towns was as follows :—*

Manchester, (population 340,211 in 1882), 131 per million.
Leeds ......   „   315,998   „   119   „
Brighton ...   „   109,595   „   114   „
Bradford ...   „   200,158   „   104   „
Oldham ...   „   115,572   „   89   „

Of course there are many other towns which have a much higher mortality, but very few are

---

* These figures have been thus obtained—the Registrar-General's Summary, 1882, (Table 7, p. xv.) gives the Small-pox deaths per 1,000, for twenty great Towns, for the years 1872-82. The Parliamentary Return, "Vaccination, Mortality," 1877, gives the Small-pox mortality and population of a considerable number of towns for the years 1847-72. From these two official papers the Small-pox mortality per million of the whole male population from 1860 to 1882, for such towns as occur in both the tables, is easily obtained. The average Small-pox death-rate for all England is found to be 211·7, while that of the ages 15—55 is 176. These numbers are in the proportion of 1 to ·83 ; hence the total Small-pox mortality of any town multiplied by the factor ·83 will give, approximately, the mortality at ages 15—45. The proportion has been obtained from males only, but that of the two sexes combined will not be materially different.

much worse than the Navy. The very worst large town which I can find in the Reports is Newcastle-on-Tyne, which for the same period had an adult Small-pox mortality of 349 per million. But the fact that five of our most populous towns have considerably less adult Small-pox mortality than the Navy, and one of them but little more than the Army, amounts to a demonstration of the uselessness of the most complete re-vaccination.

The general mortality of our adult population is much greater than that of the Army and Navy. From the official sources of information already quoted, I find that the average mortality of the adult male population of England, of the ages 15—55, for the years 1860-82, was about 11,300 per million.*

That of the Navy, for the same period, was 11,000 per million from all causes, and only 7,150 from disease.

That of the Army, at home, was 10,300 per million. Abroad it was nearly double (19,400), but this included all the deaths from casualties, exposure, &c., in the Abyssinian, Afghan, Zulu, Transvaal, and other petty wars.

* Taken from p. lii., 45th Report of the Registrar-General. —ED.

Thus the superior physique of our soldiers and sailors, together with the sanitary conditions under which they live, are fully manifested in a mortality from disease much below that of the adult civil population of comparable ages. If we make the same allowance for the influence of these causes in the case of Small-pox, there remains absolutely nothing for the alleged protective influence of re-vaccination.

Surely we shall now hear no more of the re-vaccinated nurses in Small-pox hospitals, (as to whom we have no statistics, but only vague and usually inaccurate assertions,) when we have a great, officially recorded experiment to refer to, extending over 23 years and applied to more than 200,000 men, the results of which directly contradict every professional and official statement as to the safeguard of re-vaccination.

Vaccination itself a cause of Disease and Death.

As has been now shown, vaccination is quite powerless either to prevent or to mitigate Small-pox. But this is not all, for there are good grounds for believing that it is itself the cause of much disease and serious mortality.

It was long denied by medical men that syphilis can be communicated by vaccination ; but this is now universally admitted, and no less than 478 cases of vaccine-syphilis have already been recorded.* But there is also good reason to believe that many other blood-diseases are transmitted and increased by the same means, since there has been for many years a steady increase of mortality from such diseases which is terrible to contemplate. The following table gives the increase of five of these diseases from the Registrar-General's Annual Report for 1880, (page lxxix., Table 34,) and it is very noteworthy that, in the long list of maladies there tabulated, no others, (except Bronchitis, which often follows vaccination though not, probably, transmitted by it,) show any such striking and continuous increase, while the great majority are either stationary or decreasing.

---

* See MR. TEBB's "Compulsory Vaccination in England," p. 25, (Note,) for a list of the authorities for these cases.

ANNUAL DEATHS IN ENGLAND PER MILLION LIVING.*

AVERAGE OF 5 YEARS.	1850-4	1855-9	1860-4	1865-9	1870-4	1875-9	1880.
Small-pox	279	199	191	148	433	82	25
Syphilis	37	51	64	82	81	86	84
Cancer	302	327	369	404	442	493	516
Tabes Mesenterica	265	261	272	316	299	330	371
Pyæmia, &c.	20	18	24	23	29	39	—
Skin Disease	12	15	16	17	18	23	22
Totals...	636	672	745	842	869	971	993
Progressive Increase	0	36	109	206	233	335	357

We here see a constant increase in the
mortality from each of these diseases, an
increase which in the sum of them is steady
and continuous. It is true, we have not, and
cannot have, direct proof that vaccination is
the sole cause of this increase, but we have
good reason to believe that it is the chief
cause. In the first place it is a *vera causa*,
since it directly inoculates infants and adults,
on an enormous scale, with whatever blood-
disease may exist unsuspected in the system

---

* This Table has not been continued in later Reports; but we find
that Cancer (the only disease of the five separately tabulated) goes on
steadily increasing, the mortality for the five years, 1881-85, being given in
the 48th Report as follows:—Syphilis, 92; Cancer, 544. Small-pox,
for the same period was 78.—ED.

of the infants from whom the vaccine virus is taken. In the next place, no other adequate cause has been adduced for the remarkably continuous increase of these special diseases, which the spread of sanitation, of cleanliness, and of advanced medical knowledge, should have rendered both less frequent and less fatal.

The *increased deaths from these five causes, from* 1855 *to* 1880, *exceed the total deaths from Small-pox during the same period !* So that even if the latter disease had been totally abolished by vaccination, the general mortality would have been increased, and there is much reason to believe that the increase may have been caused by vaccination itself.*

---

* It has been boldly asserted by the Government Department controlling vaccination, [Eleventh Report of the Medical Officer to Local Government Board, p. vi., et seq.,] that even if some children are killed by vaccination, 12,000 lives are annually saved by it. The basis of that assertion is *an estimate* which contradicts the official vaccination returns at almost every point. · The estimate and assertion are false to the facts which are obtainable.

The above noted estimate is taken to prove that 94 per cent. of London children under ten years of age are vaccinated, and that 95 per cent. of the population [p. 41] are vaccinated. This statement is further assumed to be supported by an examination of "53,185 children in various national, charitable, and parochial schools and workhouses in London." Such is the odious rigour of vaccine regulations in our "national, charitable, and parochial workhouse schools," that I should not have been surprised if, of these children, not one was found unvaccinated. The parents of these

poor children have had no one to defend them by paying fines for neglect
of the vaccination.   Yet this "inspection" showed 6 per cent. to have
" no vaccination scar," or to be doubtful as to vaccination.

It is on such bases, that tremendous statements, such as that noted
above, are founded ; and to shade off the impudence of this one it is further
declared that "the estimate of the number of the unvaccinated is probably
too high."   Our responsible ministers have been appealed to respecting
such a base use of official reports, and have had the humour to refer the
objector to the very officials who have so degraded their department of
"the public service."   These, in turn, when appealed to, refer to the
head of the department; meanwhile the false statement is repeatedly
quoted, and stands as first used.

The Reports of the Local Government Board, show that only once
have there ever been more than 87 per cent. of the births of the country
vaccinated, and in London 3 or 4 per cent. fewer.   The last year
reported, 1886, gives 30,000 fewer official vaccinations than 1877, when
it was over 86 per cent. of the births.   The plan of the officials is
to get 94 per cent. vaccinated, by deducting the infants who died unvaccinated from the total births, and treating the rest as *"surviving."*
I know no more condemnable trick.   Death is as busy with vaccinated
as with unvaccinated children.—ED.

PART II.

Comparative Mortality of the Vaccinated and the Unvaccinated.

IN his speech in the House of Commons, June 19th, 1883, SIR LYON PLAYFAIR made the following statement : — "An analysis of 10,000 cases in the Metropolitan Hospitals shows that 45 per cent. of the Unvaccinated patients die, and only 15 per cent. of Vaccinated patients ;" and he further showed that statistics of a similar character had been published in other countries. It will no doubt be objected by my readers that these statistics, if correct, are a complete proof of the value of vaccination ; and I shall be expected to show that they are incorrect or give up the whole case. This I am prepared to do ; and I now undertake to prove— firstly, that the figures here given are unreliable ; and, secondly, that such statistics *necessarily* give false results unless they are classified according to the age-periods of the patients.

The per-centages of Vaccinated and Unvaccinated unreliable.

The simple fact of death from Small-pox is easily ascertained, and has been for many years accurately recorded.

But, whether the deceased person had been vaccinated or not, is a fact by no means easily ascertained, because confluent Small-pox (which alone is ordinarily fatal) obliterates the vaccination marks in the worst cases, and the death is then usually recorded among the unvaccinated or the doubtful. For this reason alone the official record—*vaccinated* or *unvaccinated*—is altogether untrustworthy, and cannot be made the subject of accurate statistical enquiry.*

But there are other reasons why the comparison of the deaths of these two classes is worthless. Deaths registered as *unvaccinated* include—

(1.)—Infants dying under vaccination age, and who, therefore, have no corresponding class among

---

* As an instance of the reticence of officials on the subject. I cannot find any details in the Registrar-General's reports respecting vaccinated persons dying of Small-pox until 1874. For that year 270 vaccinated persons are reported dying of Small-pox. Then for years no information is given, until 1879, when it is again inserted. For that and the subsequent years we have 2,512 vaccinated persons returned as dying of Small-pox. Several thousands are noted as "not stated as to vaccination."—ED.

the vaccinated, but among whom the Small-pox
mortality is greatest.

(2.) –Children too weakly or diseased to be
vaccinated, and whose low vitality renders any
severe disease fatal.

(3.)—A large but unknown number of the
criminal and nomad population who escape
the vaccination officers. These are often badly
fed and live under the most unsanitary conditions ;
they are, therefore, especially liable to suffer in
epidemics of Small-pox or other zymotic diseases.

It is by the indiscriminate union of these
three classes, together with those erroneously
classed as unvaccinated owing to the obliteration
of marks or other defect of evidence, that the
number of deaths registered "*unvaccinated*" is
swollen far beyond its true proportions, and the
comparison with those registered "*vaccinated*"
rendered altogether untrustworthy and misleading.

This is not a mere inference, for there is much
direct evidence that the records "unvaccinated"
and "no statement" in the Reports of the
Registrar-General are often erroneous. As the
chief argument for vaccination rests upon this
class of facts, a few examples of the evidence
referred to must be here given.

(1.)—Mr. A. Feltrup, of Ipswich, gives a case of a boy aged 9, who died of Small-pox, and was recorded in the certificate as "unvaccinated." By a search in the register of successful vaccinations it was found that the boy, Thomas Taylor, had been successfully vaccinated on the 20th May, 1868, by W. Adams. (*Suffolk Chronicle*, May 5, 1877.)

(2.)—In "Notes on the Small-pox Epidemic at Birkenhead, 1877." By Fras. Vacher, M.D., (p. 9.,) we find the following :—

"As regards the patients admitted to the fever hospital or treated at home, those entered as vaccinated displayed undoubted cicatrices, as attested by competent medical witnesses, and those entered as not vaccinated were admitted unvaccinated or without the faintest mark. *The mere assertions of patients or their friends that they were vaccinated counted for nothing, as about 80 per cent. of the patients entered in the third column of the table* ('unknown') *were reported as having been vaccinated in infancy.*" (The italics are my own.)

(3.)—Bearing upon this important admission, we have the following statement in Dr. Russell's Glasgow Report, 1871-2 (p. 25) :—

"Sometimes persons were said to be vaccinated,

but no marks could be seen, very frequently because of the abundance of the eruption. In some cases of those which recovered, an inspection before dismissal discovered vaccine marks, sometimes 'very good,'"

(4.)—"The last epidemic of Small-pox which visited vaccinated Preston was in 1877. In February of that year, Dr. Rigby, the medical officer of the Union, sent out a report, in which he stated that 'out of 83 persons admitted into the Fulwood Small-pox Hospital, 73 were vaccinated.' All recovered, he alleged, but the ten unvaccinated cases all died. Here was a bold and specific statement; but what were the facts revealed after careful investigation by two committees? The first case reported as unvaccinated turned out to be *a revaccinated policeman*, named Walter Egan. Another case reported as unvaccinated was a child named Mary Shorrock, *vaccinated by the very medical officer who returned her as unvaccinated.* In all, six cases out of the ten were proved to have been vaccinated, whilst three were doubtful, we not being able to trace them."—From letter of Mr. J. SWINDLEHURST, in the *Walsall Observer*, July 21st, 1888.—ED.

(5.)—In 1872, MR. JOHN PICKERING, of Leeds, carefully investigated a number of cases entered as "not vaccinated" by the medical officers of the Leeds Small-pox Hospital, tracing out the parents, examining the patients if alive, or obtaining the certificate of vaccination if they were dead. The result was, that 6 patients, entered as "not vaccinated," and still living, were found to have good vaccination marks; while 9 others who had died, and whose deaths had been registered as "not vaccinated," were proved to have been successfully vaccinated. In addition to these, 8 cases were proved to have been vaccinated, some of them three or four times, but unsuccessfully, and 4 others were certified "unfit to be vaccinated," yet all were alike entered as "unvaccinated." The full particulars of this investigation are to be found in a pamphlet by MR. PICKERING, published by F. PITMAN, 20, Paternoster Row, London.

(6.)—As further corroborative evidence of the untrustworthiness of all records on the subject emanating from medical men, the following quotation from an article on "Certificates of Death," in the *Birmingham Medical Review* for January, 1874, is important; the italics are my own :—" In certificates given by us voluntarily, and to which the public have access, it is scarcely to be expected that a medical man will give opinions which may tell against or reflect upon himself in any way. In such cases he will most likely tell the truth, *but not the whole truth*, and assign some prominent symptom of the disease as the cause of death. As instances of cases which may tell against the medical man himself, I will mention *erysipelas from vaccination*, and puerperal fever. A death from the first cause occurred not long ago in my practice, and although I had not vaccinated the child, yet *in my desire to preserve vaccination from reproach, I omitted all mention of it from my certificate of death.*"

The illustrative facts now given cannot be supposed to be exceptional, especially when we consider the great amount of time and labour required to bring them to light; and taken in connection with the astounding admissions of medical men, of which examples have been just given, they prove that *no dependence can be placed on the official records of the proportions of vaccinated and unvaccinated among Small-pox patients;* while, if MR. VACHER's method of registration is usually followed, about 80 per cent. of those classed by the Registrar-General under the heading "no statement" have been really stated, by their parents or friends, to have been vaccinated.

OUR HOSPITAL STATISTICS NECESSARILY GIVE FALSE RESULTS.

But a still more serious matter remains to be considered, and it is a striking proof of the crude and imperfect evidence on which the important question of the value of vaccination has been decided, that the point in question has been entirely overlooked by every English advocate of vaccination, although it involves an elementary principle of statistical science.

This point is, that until the records in our hospitals, "vaccinated" and "unvaccinated," are strictly correct, and properly classified, it can be demonstrated that true results cannot be deduced from them.*

The requisite comparison has, however, been made on a population of about 60,000, consisting of the officials and workmen employed on the Imperial Austrian State Railways, by the Head Physician, DR. LEANDER JOSEPH KELLER; and his results during the years 1872-3 are so important that it is necessary to give a brief abstract of them.†

---

* See remarks in the Appendix on the eruption.—ED.

† Report on Small-pox cases among the Employés of the Imperial Austrian State Railway Company for the year 1873. Translated from the German by MRS. HUME-ROTHERY. National Anti-Compulsory Vaccination League.

Another and enlarged version of DR. KELLER'S Report has been published:
The Mitigation Theory of Vaccination: an Account of the Statistics collected during the Small-pox Epidemic of 1872-73; By DR. KELLER, Medical Director of the Austrian State Railways. By ALFRED MILNES, M.A.—London: E. W. ALLEN, Ave Maria Lane.

(1.)—It is shown that the death-rate of Small-pox patients is greatest in the first year of life, then diminishes gradually to between the 15th and 20th year, and then rises again to old age ; *thus following exactly the same law as the general mortality.*

(2.)—The Small-pox death-rate, among over 2,000 cases, was 17·85 per cent. of the cases, closely agreeing with the general average. That of the unvaccinated was 23·20 per cent., while that of the vaccinated was only 15·61 per cent.

(3.)—This result, apparently so favourable to vaccination, is shown to be wholly due to the excess of the unvaccinated in the first two years of life,* and to be *a purely numerical fact entirely unconnected with vaccination.* This is proved as follows :—Taking, first, all the ages above 2 years, the death-rates of the vaccinated is 13·76, and of the unvaccinated 13·15,— almost exactly the same, but with a slight advantage to the unvaccinated.

Taking now the first two years, the death-rate is found to be as follows :—

	Vaccinated.	Unvaccinated.
First year of life	60·46	45·24
Second year of life	54·05	38·10

* This applies to Austria. In England vaccination is usually performed earlier, yet, in a pamphlet entitled "*Plain Facts on Vaccination,*" by

Thus the Small-pox death-rate is actually *less* for the unvaccinated than for the vaccinated in infants, and *equal* for all the higher ages; yet the average of the whole is higher for the unvaccinated, *simply on account of the greater proportion of the unvaccinated at those ages at which the mortality is universally greatest.*

It is thus made clear that any comparison of the Small-pox mortality of the vaccinated and the unvaccinated, *except at strictly corresponding ages,* leads to entirely false conclusions.

This curious and important fact may perhaps be rendered more easily intelligible by an illustration. Let us take the whole population up to 20 years of age, and divide it into two groups—those who go to school, and those who do not. If the Small-pox mortality of these were separately registered, it would be found to be very much greater among the non-school goers,—composed chiefly of infants, and of children too weakly to be sent to school, amongst whom the mortality is always very

---

G. OLIVER, about 1872, it was stated that in the Small-pox Hospital, Hampstead,—"The number of the unvaccinated patients, up to the age of ten years, greatly preponderates over the vaccinated of corresponding ages." In the Homerton Small-pox Hospital in the eight years 1871-77, there were 147 unvaccinated patients under 2 years old, to 20 vaccinated, including among these the doubtful cases.

great, so much so that a doctor of wide experience—DR. VERNON, of Southport—has stated
that, he had never known an infant under one year
of age recover from Small-pox.   But we should
surely think a person either silly or mad who
argued from such statistics that school-going was
a protection against the disease, and that school
children formed a "protected population."   Yet
this is exactly comparable with the reasoning
of those who adduce the greater mortality among
unvaccinated Small-pox patients of all ages
and conditions, as the very strongest argument
in favour of vaccination !

Good statistics * and good arguments cannot
be upset, or even weakened, by those which are
bad.   I have now shown that the main argument
relied on by our adversaries, rests on thoroughly
unsound statistics, inaccurate to begin with, and
wrongly interpreted afterwards.   Those which I
have used, on the other hand, if not absolutely
perfect, are yet the best and most trustworthy
that exist.   I ask statisticians and men of
unbiassed judgment to decide between them.

---

* It must be insisted upon, over and over again, that they are not good
statistics, where the class under trial—the vaccinated—are in great numbers
of cases assumed not to be vaccinated against all testimony available.—ED.

CONCLUSION FROM THE EVIDENCE.

The result of this brief enquiry may be thus summarized :—

(1.)—Vaccination does not diminish Small-pox mortality, as shown by the 45 years of the Registrar-General's statistics, and by the deaths from Small-pox of our "re-vaccinated" soldiers and sailors being as numerous as those of the male population of the same ages of several of our large towns, although the former are picked, healthy men, while the latter include many thousands living under the most unsanitary conditions.

(2.)—While thus utterly powerless for good, vaccination * is a certain cause of disease and death in many cases, and is the probable cause of about 10,000 deaths annually by five inocu-lable diseases of the most terrible and disgusting character, which have increased to this extent, steadily, year by year, since vaccination has been enforced by penal laws!

(3.)—The hospital statistics, showing a greater

---

* The operation itself kills many. The Registrar-General gives, under the head of Cow-pox and other effects [erysipelas, &c.] of vaccination for the years 1881 to 1886, the following deaths of infants under one year. In the country, 255 deaths. In London, 61. Total for the six years, 316.—ED,

mortality of the unvaccinated than of the vaccinated, have been proved to be untrustworthy;
while the conclusions drawn from them are
shown to be necessarily false.

If these facts are true, or anything near the
truth, the enforcement of vaccination by fine
and imprisonment of unwilling parents, is a
cruel and criminal despotism, which it behoves
all true friends of humanity to denounce and
oppose at every opportunity.

Such legislation, involving as it does, our
health, our liberty, and our very lives, is too
serious a matter to be allowed to depend on
the misstatements of interested officials or the
dogmas of a professional clique. Some of the
misstatements and some of the ignorance on
which you have relied, have been here
exposed. The statistical evidence on which
alone a true judgment can be founded, is
as open to you as to any doctor in the
land. We, therefore, demand that you, our
representatives, shall fulfil your solemn duty
to us in this matter, by devoting to it
some personal investigation and painstaking
research ; and if you find that the main facts

as here stated are substantially correct, we
call upon you to undo without delay the evil
you have done.

WE, THEREFORE, SOLEMNLY URGE UPON YOU
THE IMMEDIATE REPEAL OF THE INIQUITOUS
PENAL LAWS BY WHICH YOU HAVE FORCED UPON
US A DANGEROUS AND USELESS OPERATION—AN
OPERATION WHICH HAS ADMITTEDLY CAUSED MANY
DEATHS, WHICH IS PROBABLY THE CAUSE OF
GREATER MORTALITY THAN SMALL-POX ITSELF,
BUT WHICH CANNOT BE PROVED TO HAVE EVER
SAVED A SINGLE HUMAN LIFE.

APPENDIX.

IN addition to other difficulties besetting the students of our Hospital records, one stands prominently forward as exceeding the others. DR. WALLACE has referred to the difficulty of comparing vaccinated with those called un-vaccinated, who are a mixed class, often not even classed in age together. But a greater omission must be complained of.

The only correct way of classing Small-pox patients is by age and by eruption. The eruption, or the state of the skin, is the only scientific guide to the nature of the disorder. One kind of Small-pox is so mild, that even bad nursing can hardly kill the patient—another kind so fatal, that not the best nursing and greatest skill can cure it. As a rule these two kinds are lumped together without any distinction, and even when given they are not often divided into vaccinated and un-vaccinated. In general summaries this classification is universally disregarded.

The Metropolitan Hospitals have been in operation since 1869. During the 16 years reported upon to the managers, since that time they have received 53,579 cases of Small-pox for treatment. Of this great total, no fewer than 41,061 are classed as vaccinated, 5,866 un-vaccinated, and the remainder as "doubtful." The fatality of the un-vaccinated and doubtful is very heavy, but this is largely due to considerations as to the people who are the un-vaccinated, which have already been urged, and which are greatly strengthened by facts now to be adduced.

The Handbook, 1887, giving these particulars, has no "doubtful" class until 1880. Before that period the un-vaccinated absorbed them all.

As to this doubtful class! Why are there any doubts in the classification? The answer is that the vaccination marks are on the skin, and the skin is the part of the patient most affected in the very bad cases. In the mild cases the skin does not suffer much. The vaccination marks are clearly visible. And so the "good" marks of vaccination will most certainly be most numerous in the mild cases. But in the confluent cases the skin is badly affected. The pustules run together, and if this eruption is over the vaccinated arm, no vaccination mark can be seen. But no case is recorded as vaccinated unless a mark is seen. So it comes to pass, that such a patient declaring himself vaccinated is put down as "doubtful," or as "said to be vaccinated." We see now why this class is of heavy fatality. It receives the doubtful bad cases, but never any doubtful mild ones.

This is further confirmed by a reference to the most fatal cases of all, the "malignant." In these the skin is not degraded as it is in the confluent; the eruption is suppressed, and the blood poisoned. But the vaccination marks show. From several reports of medical super-intendants, I have collected 661 of these very fatal cases. In only 8 cases were there "doubts." The rest yield: vaccinated, 486 persons with 432 deaths; and un-vaccinated, 167 persons with 150 deaths. Nothing more damaging to vaccination could be recorded. Yet in a purely age table; or in a table of vaccinated and un-vaccinated, without reference to the state of the skin, all this is buried.

We see then that in the mild cases, error as to classification is very unlikely ever to occur. In these no deaths need be feared, except from complications.

WORKS BY THE SAME AUTHOR.

THE MALAY ARCHIPELAGO: The land of the Orang Utan and the Bird of Paradise. A Narrative of Travel, with Studies of Man and Nature. With Maps and Illustrations. Third and Cheaper Edition. Crown 8vo. 7s. 6d.

"The result is a vivid picture of tropical life, which may be read with unflagging interest, and a sufficient account of his scientific conclusions to stimulate our appetite without wearying us by detail. In short, we may safely say that we have never read a more agreeable book of its kind."—*Saturday Review.*

THE GEOGRAPHICAL DISTRIBUTION OF ANIMALS. With a Study of the Relations of Living and Extinct Faunas as Elucidating the Past Changes of the Earth's Surface. 2 vols. 8vo., with Maps and numerous Illustrations by ZWECKER. 42s.

The *Times* says:—"Altogether it is a wonderful and fascinating story, whatever objections may be taken to theories founded upon it. Mr. Wallace has not attempted to add to its interest by any adornments of style; he has given a simple and clear statement of intrinsically interesting facts, and what he considers to be legitimate deductions from them. Naturalists ought to be grateful to him for having undertaken so toilsome a task. The work, indeed, is a credit to all concerned—the author, the publishers, the artist, unfortunately now no more, of the attractive illustrations—last, but by no means least, Mr. Stanford's map-designer."

TROPICAL NATURE: With other Essays. 8vo. 12s.

"Nowhere amid the many descriptions of the tropics that have been given is to be found a summary of the past history and actual phenomena of the tropics which gives that which is distinctive of the phases of nature in them more clearly, shortly, and impressively."—*Saturday Review.*

ISLAND LIFE; OR, THE PHENOMENA AND CAUSES OF INSULAR FAUNAS AND FLORAS, including a Revision and attempted Solution of the Problem of Geological Climates. With Maps. 8vo. 18s.

"'Island Life' is a work to be accepted almost without reservation from beginning to end. . . Whoever reads this book must be charmed with it."—*St. James's Gazette.*
"The work throughout abounds with interest."—*Athenæum.*
"Mr. Wallace has written nothing more clear, more masterly, or more convincing than this delightful volume."—*Fortnightly Review.*

BAD TIMES: An Essay on the Present Depression of Trade, tracing it to its Sources in Enormous Foreign Loans, Excessive War Expenditure, the Increase of Speculation and of Millionaires, and the Depopulation of the Rural Districts; with Suggested Remedies. 1885. With Diagrams. Crown 8vo. 5s.

LONDON: MACMILLAN & CO.

LAND NATIONALISATION, ITS NECESSITY AND ITS AIMS. Being a comparison of the System of Landlord and Tenant with that of Occupying Ownership in their influence on the Well-being of the People. Third Edition. Paper covers, 8d. Limp cloth, 1s. 6d.

LONDON: W. REEVES, 185, FLEET STREET, E.C.

ON MIRACLES AND MODERN SPIRITUALISM.

Three Essays. Second Edition, crown 8vo., cloth, 5s.

LONDON: TRUBNER & CO., LUDGATE HILL.

The London Society for
The Abolition of Compulsory Vaccination.

President.
WILLIAM TEBB, Esq., 7, Albert Road, Gloucester Gate, Regent's Park, N.W.

Vice-Presidents.
THOMAS BURT, Esq., M.P., 26, Palace Street, Buckingham Gate, S.W.
HENRY P. COBB, Esq., M.P., 53, Lincoln's-Inn Fields, W.C.
HANDEL COSSHAM, Esq., M.P., Weston Park, Bath.
ISAAC HOLDEN, Esq., M.P., Oakworth House, Keighley.

Executive Committee.
CHAIRMAN.—WILLIAM TEBB.

R. ALFREY.	GENERAL EARLE.	JOHN LEWIS.
W. L. BEURLE.	Mrs. R. R. GLOVER.	Mrs. LOWE.
JOHN BOTTOMLEY.	J. F. HAINES.	CORNELIUS PEARSON.

WILLIAM WHITE, Laurels, Cheshunt, Herts.

Hon. Treasurer—CORNELIUS PEARSON, 15, Harpur Street, Red Lion Square, W.C.
Bankers—THE LONDON & COUNTY BANK (Westminster Branch), S.W.
Parliamentary Agent—W. L. BEURLE, Linden House, 331, Victoria Park Road, E.
Secretary—WILLIAM YOUNG, 77, Atlantic Road, Brixton, S.W.

IN times when the laws of health were imperfectly understood, it was believed that by poisoning the blood with the virus of small-pox, or cow-pox, a future attack of small-pox might be escaped. While many kindred medical practices have been discredited and forgotten, Vaccination, endowed by the State, has survived, and has entered into legislation, and is enforced with fine and imprisonment. It is in vain for nonconformists to plead that they do not believe that Vaccination has any power to prevent or to mitigate small-pox, or that it is attended by the risk of communicating other diseases. They are told they may believe what they like, but that vaccinated they must be, for the benefit of the rite is settled beyond dispute, and that only fools and fanatics venture to question what has been irrevocably determined.

Many too, whilst disinclined to discuss Vaccination as a medical question, or to surrender confidence in its prophylaxy, are opposed to its compulsory infliction. They maintain that every remedy should be left to justify itself by its own efficacy, and that of all prescriptions the last which requires extraneous assistance is Vaccination; for its repute is based on the fact that its subjects are secure from small-pox, and in that security may abide indifferent to those who choose to neglect its salvation. Even nurses in small-pox hospitals, it is said, when efficiently vaccinated and re-vaccinated, live unaffected in the variolous atmosphere. They consequently hold that to compare an unvaccinated person to a nuisance, as is frequently done, is to make use of an epithet that implicitly denies the virtues asserted for Vaccination, a nuisance being a danger or annoyance which another cannot conveniently avoid.

The members of the LONDON SOCIETY therefore appeal with confidence to the sympathy and support of their countrymen. They claim to enlist the energies not only of those who are opposed to Vaccination as useless and mischievous, but of those who, true to their faith in liberty, would leave its acceptance to the discretion of the individual.

THE LONDON SOCIETY FOR
THE ABOLITION OF COMPULSORY VACCINATION.

OBJECTS OF THE SOCIETY.

I.—The Abolition of Compulsory Vaccination.

II.—The Diffusion of Knowledge concerning Vaccination.

III.—The Maintenance in London of an Office for the Publication of Literature relating to Vaccination, and a Centre of Information and Action.

The minimum Annual Subscription constituting Membership is 2s. 6d. Every opponent of Compulsory Vaccination in the United Kingdom is earnestly invited to join and co-operate with the Society.

I AM directed to draw attention very earnestly to the claims of the London Society for the Abolition of Compulsory Vaccination.

The Society is engaged in an arduous enterprise with the firm resolve to achieve success; and with this end in view the Members maintain an Office; they publish the *Vaccination Inquirer*, and a variety of books, tracts, and leaflets, which are liberally distributed wherever likely to be of use; they organise public meetings, and avail themselves of every opportunity for lectures and discussions; and from the Office conduct an extensive correspondence at home and abroad.

It is needless to say that all these operations are attended with expense, and indeed with heavy expense, yet from none of them is it possible to withdraw; on the contrary with larger means they would be developed and extended. At present the chief cost of these operations is borne by the liberality of the few, and it is the wish, and the reasonable wish, of the Committee to enlarge the area of subscription, and to have the names of all opponents of Compulsory Vaccination upon their register of membership.

The successful issue of this most honourable agitation would be greatly hastened if only those who are persuaded of the folly of vaccination, and who abhor the tyrannical infliction of the rite upon the unwilling, would come forward and assist to sustain those who are disposed to assume the more active duties of the conflict. The Committee feel that it is not becoming that many, who have openly expressed their sympathy with the objects they have in view, and who will rejoice over the Abolition of Compulsory Vaccination, should yet do little or nothing to contribute to the victory which they are sufficiently enlightened to desire.

The Committee therefore hope that you will not only look favourably on this appeal for assistance, but that you will also try to enlist in the good cause some of those latent sympathisers, who, probably, only require the stimulus of suggestion and persuasion to become active allies.

WILLIAM YOUNG,
Secretary.

77, ATLANTIC ROAD,
BRIXTON, S.W.

THE VACCINATION INQUIRER.

Published Monthly, price 1d., or 1s. 6d. per annum, post free.

E. W. ALLEN, 4 AVE MARIA LANE, LONDON, E.C.

www.ingramcontent.com/pod-product-compliance
Lightning Source LLC
Chambersburg PA
CBHW021553270326
41931CB00009B/1191

* 9 7 8 3 3 3 7 5 6 5 0 3 9 *